How To V
Poetry & Stories

Grades 4-6

Written by Vi Clarke & Leona Melnyk
Illustrated by S&S Learning Materials

ISBN 1-55035-216-4
Copyright 1991
Revised January 2006
All Rights Reserved · Printed in Canada

Published in the United States by:
On the Mark Press
3909 Witmer Road PMB 175
Niagara Falls, New York
14305
www.onthemarkpress.com

Published in Canada by:
S&S Learning Materials
15 Dairy Avenue
Napanee, Ontario
K7R 1M4
www.sslearning.com

Look For Other Language Units

POETRY AND CREATIVE WRITING

Table of Contents

Poetry

Creative Writing

© 1991 S&S Learning Materials Limited.

POETRY AND CREATIVE WRITING

Teacher Input Suggestions

1. Display many books of poems, funny and serious, around the classroom. Perhaps set up a poetry corner.

2. Read different kinds of poetry, both serious and humorous, to your students each day.

3. Have a "poem of the month" contest. Have each student find a poem for each particular month, or perhaps they could find seasonal poems. After reciting poems, students vote on the one they like best. Perhaps a class mural, sculpture, or other project could be done about the poem.

4. Have students find a poem they like and then look through old magazines, travel brochures, catalogs, etc. for a picture to go with their poems. These can be attractively mounted around the classroom.

5. Have students design greeting cards for classmates or relatives to send on birthdays or other special occasions. They can fold a piece of unlined white paper horizontally or vertically down the center. On the inside, students can write a favorite or original poem. Decorate the outside using markers, tissue paper, colored pencils, etc.

6. Listen to tapes and/or records of students' favorite songs for rhyming lyrics.

7. Display students' poems in a class book or, if your school has a newspaper, publish typed poems. Perhaps you could submit poems to children's magazines.

8. Have students write rhyming jingles for a television commercial. Food is a good topic for such jingles.

9. Have students create a shoe box poetry diorama based on an original or favorite poem. Paint the outside of the box, or cover it with construction paper. Inside the box, place scenery,

people, animals, furniture, etc. made from clay, sticks, paper, and other materials. Cover with plastic wrap when finished. Tape a neatly written copy of the poem to the side of the box.

10. Make a bulletin board display of the ingredients of a story-

    1) characters (mount pictures of people, animals, etc.)
    2) setting (pictures of houses, landscape, etc.)
    3) problem (pictures of storms, fires, fog, flat tire, etc.)
    4) climax (someone being rescued)
    5) ending (Cut last pages of books.)

    Have students write stories and put them on display.

11. Make a bulletin board display "Poems - the Most for the Least". Display samples of limericks, cinquains, haiku and other types of poetry written by students.

12. Throughout the unit, make use of a proofreading code that you and/or your students devise or the one which follows.

    SP   Spelling mistakes.

    --->   Start new paragraph.

    C   Add a capital letter.

    P   Add necessary punctuation.

    ^   A letter or word has been left out.

    ?   This does not make sense to me.

    " "   Quotation marks needed.

POETIC POWER!

Activity 1

Poetic Expression

Poetry is a form of literary expression. The poet tries to convey his moods feelings and ideas in a very beautiful lyrical fashion. A good poet taps the reader's senses. He is able to create a picture in the mind's eye of the reader. The reader can almost see, hear, feel, taste or smell what the poet describes.

A   Read the following poems. Then on the chart provided tell which senses were stimulated and write the words that caused this reaction.

A Fairy Voyage

If I were just a fairy small,
I'd take a leaf and sail away,
I'd sit astride the stem and guide
It straight to Fairyland and stay.
Author Unknown

The Rain

Rain on the green grass,
And rain on the tree,
And rain on the house-top,
But not upon me!
Author Unknown

A Baby Sardine

A baby Sardine
Saw her first submarine
She was scared
And watched through a peephole.

"Oh come, come, come,"
Said the Sardine's mum,
It's only a tin full of people.
Author Unknown

White Sheep

White sheep, white sheep,
On a blue hill,
When the wind stops
You all stand still.
When the wind blows
You walk away slow.
White sheep, white sheep,
Where do you go?
Author Unknown

POETIC POWER!

Activity 1

Poetic Expression

Poems	Senses	Words that caused the reaction
1. A Fairy Voyage		
2. A Baby Sardine		
3. The Rain -		
4. White Sheep		

B Select one of the poems above and do an illustration depicting what you have read.

C Now try your hand at a poem of your very own. Try to stimulate as many senses as you can. Trade your finished poem with a partner. You read your partner's poem and then next to the "senses" shapes below write the words that stimulated that particular sense.

POETIC POWER!

Activity 1

Poetic Expression

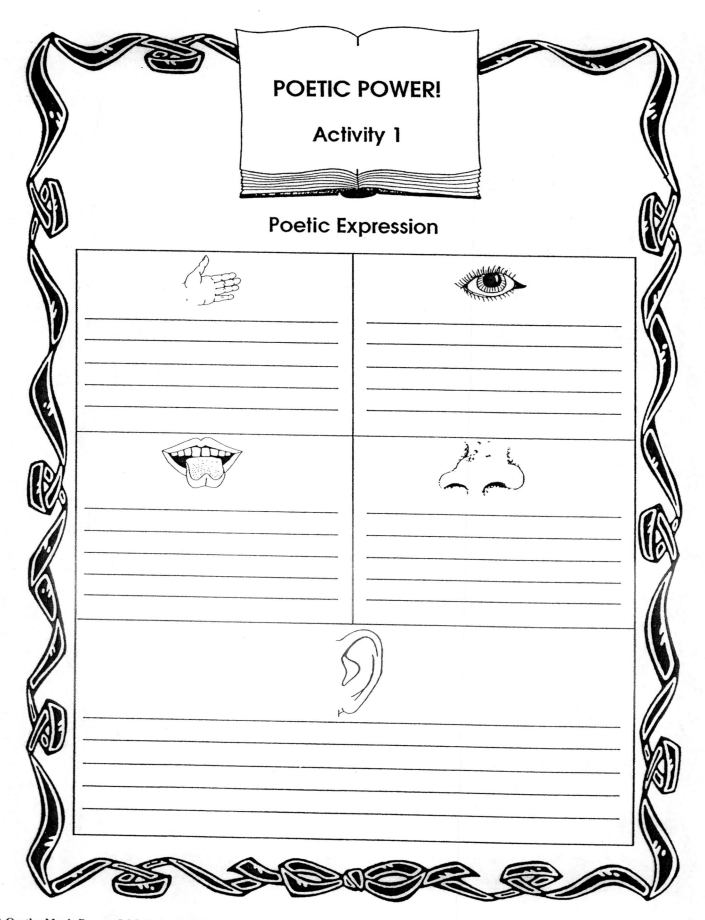

POETIC POWER!

Activity 2

Echoic Words

Onomatopoeia could be called echoic words or sound words. It is in fact, a poetic device using words whose sounds echo their meaning. For example (pop, buzz, rustle, bang)

A   Find examples of onomatopoeia in the following poem and underline them.

The Big Clock

Slowly ticks the big clock;
Tick-tock, tick-tock!
But Cuckoo clock ticks double-quick;
Tick-a-tock-a, tick-a-tock-a,
Tick-a-tock-a, tick!

Author Unknown

B   Now write a poem of your own using onomatopoeia. Underline all the sound words in your poem.

C   Illustrate a sound word of your choice. (See the samples below). Some suggested words are: ring, splash, bang, buzz.

POETIC POWER!

Activity 3

A Treasure of Similes

A simile is a figure of speech that makes a comparison using the words "like" or "as". Similes are often incorporated into poems to enhance and emphasize a certain thought. An example of a simile is: The storm roared like a raging lion. (The storm is compared to a lion)

Read the following sentences, then complete each by using a simile. In the brackets, write the two words that are compared. The first one is done for you.

1. The stars sparkled like diamonds. (stars, diamonds)

2. She is as pretty _____ .

   (_____)

3. That story is as old _____ .

   (_____)

4. The child was as curious _____ .

   (_____)

5. Her shiny hair looks like _____ .

   (_____)

6. My hot chocolate is as cold _____ .

   (_____)

POETIC POWER!

Activity 3

A Treasure of Similes

7. She is as slow _____.

(_____)

8. The injured man cried like _____.

(_____)

9. The winner was as happy _____.

(_____)

10. The angry man roared like _____.

(_____)

Now write several sentences of your own incorporating a simile in each one. Try using these sentences to make up a poem of your own. Write your poem in the treasure chest below.

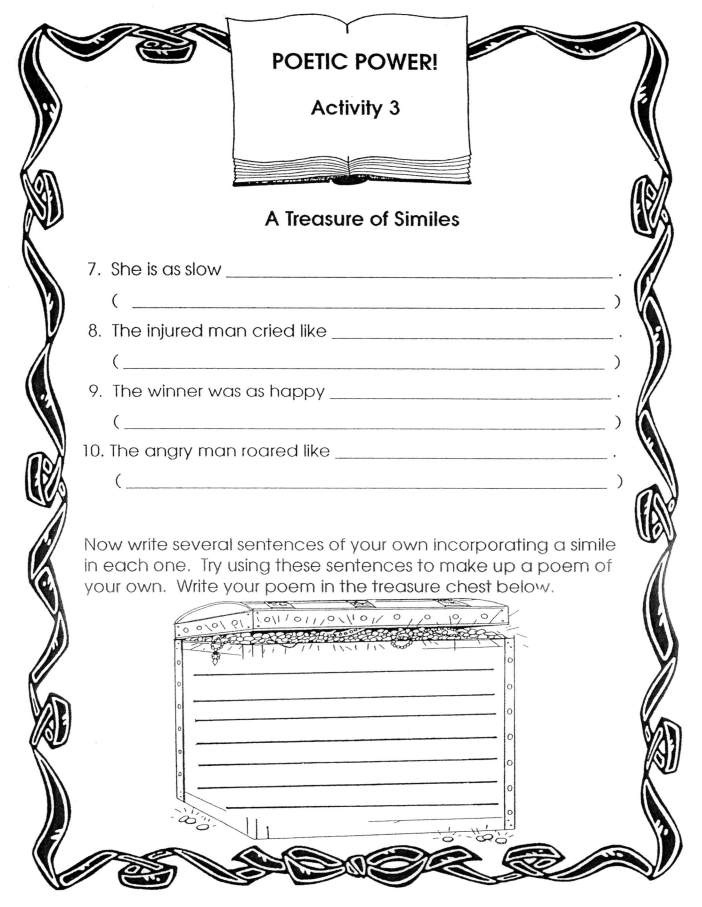

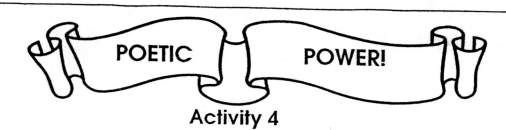

POETIC POWER!

Activity 4

Starring Metaphors

One poetic device often used in poetry is the metaphor. A metaphor is a figure of speech whereby things are compared without using like or as. For example: Happiness is sunshine from within. (Happiness is compared to sunshine).

A Complete the sentences below by using a metaphor.

1. A star is a _____ in the sky.

2. When it comes to swimming, Jane is a real _____.

3. My mother's voice is _____ to my ears.

4. A soft, fluffy cloud is a _____.

5. The snow-covered lawn is _____.

B Now try your hand at writing metaphors in sentences of your own. Write your sentences in the stars provided.

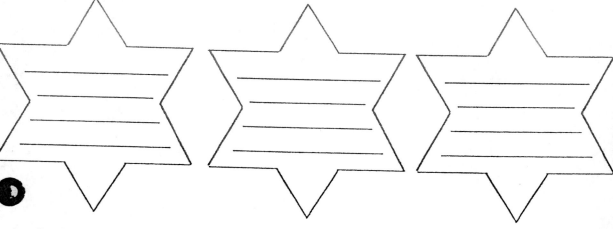

C Use your sentences to create an original poem. Be a real star and shine!

POETIC POWER!

Activity 5

Personification

Personification is the act of giving human qualities to an idea, an object or an experience. For example: The (brook) <u>laughed</u> and <u>chattered</u> as it trickled over the rocks.

Read the sentences below. Put brackets around the idea, object or experience being personified; then underline the word or words that denote human qualities.

1. Winter painted the land with a carpet of snow.

2. The waves rolled continuously against the rocky shore.

3. The airplane roared down the narrow runway.

4. The snow danced gracefully to the ground.

5. The raindrops danced on the window panes.

6. Her old shoes moaned as she ascended the stairs.

7. The door groaned as the frightened child dared to open it.

8. The neon lights winked at passers-by.

9. The daffodils danced in the breeze.

10. The birds sang their beautiful songs.

POETIC POWER!
Activity 6

Haiku

Haiku is a type of poem that originated in Japan. The Haiku poem is unrhymed. The topics chosen are usually about nature - animals, water etc. The poems create a picture in your mind or a feeling in your soul. They are simple but very effective.

Haiku consists of 3 lines.
1. Line one has 5 syllables.
2. Line two has 7 syllables.
3. Line three has 5 syllables.

Here is an example for you.

**Stars - how they sparkle
Dancing to and fro all night,
Peace and calm avails!**

Express yourself creatively by writing a Haiku poem.
Some suggested topics are:

| sand | trees | night | wind | sea | grass | ice | stars | flowers |

Write your poem below:

_____

_____

_____

_____

_____

_____

_____

_____

_____

_____

POETIC POWER!

Activity 7

Cinquains

A cinquain is a five lined poem that follows this pattern:

1st line - one word title
2nd line - two words describing the title
3rd line - three action words
4th line - four words expressing a feeling
5th line - one word that means the same as the title

Animals are good topics for cinquains. For example:

Dog
Loyal, obedient
Barks, romps, chases
A man's best friend
Canine

Cat
Independent, aloof
Mews, scratches, purrs
Loves to chase mice
Feline

You may want to write a cinquain about yourself.

Richard
Brown-eyed, freckle-faced
Reads, travels, studies
Loves to play Nintendo
Male

Sports also lend themselves well to cinquains as do colors places, planets, countries, etc. Choose a topic and write your own cinquain following the prescribed format above.

POETIC POWER!

Activity 8

Limericks

There are many kinds of humorous poetry such as nursery rhymes, riddles, tongue twisters, parodies, and limericks. Edward Lear has been called "the father of English nonsense" because of the limericks he wrote.

A limerick is a humorous five line poem in which lines 1,2, and 5 rhyme as do lines 3 and 4. Some limericks are silly and use nonsense words. Read the following two limericks by Edward Lear.

> There was a Young Lady whose chin
> Resembled the point of a pin.
> So she had it made sharp
> And purchased a harp,
> And played several tunes with her chin.

> There was an Old Man on whose nose
> Most birds of the air could repose,
> But they all flew away
> At the closing of day,
> Which relieved the Old Man and his nose.

Can you illustrate these poems? Be creative!

Now be "lear"-y and write and illustrate your own limerick.

POETIC POWER!

Activity 9

Concrete Poetry

Some poets are artists because they use a shape to give their poems more meaning. This is called concrete poetry. Below are two examples.

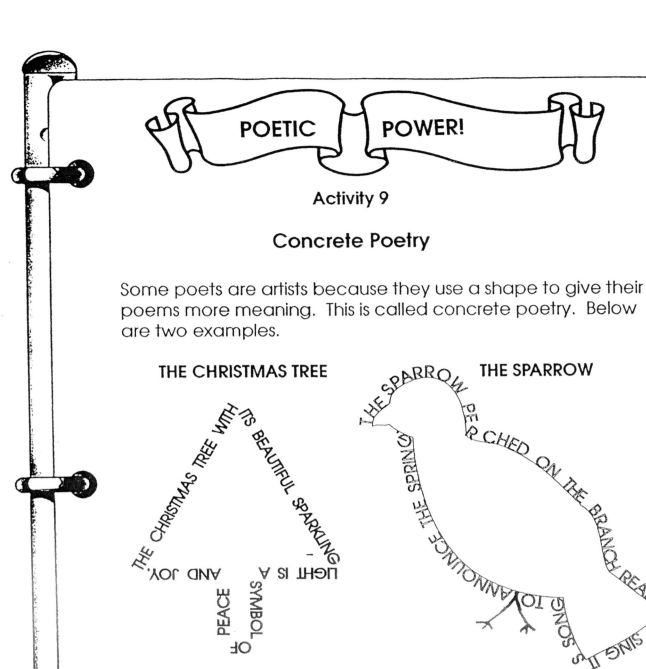

THE CHRISTMAS TREE

THE SPARROW

Some topics that lend themselves well to concrete poems are:

snake	mouse	car
boat	cat	flower
fish	tree	food

Choose one of these topics or any other that interests you and write a shapely poem.

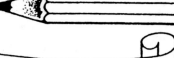

POETIC POWER!

Activity 10

Rainbow Poetry

Colors can make us see things better, like looking at the world through rose-colored glasses.

Try and find in your library books, stories, or poems about color. For example, <u>Hailstones and Halibut Bones</u> by Mary O'Neill.

Then choose seven colors and write on a rainbow shape all the ideas that those colors bring to mind. Include feelings, smells, and sounds as well as objects. For example:

Smell of burnt toast BLACK Magic Raven's wings Shiny coal
The crunch of lettuce GREEN Envy A dense forest Slippery frogs
The warmth of a fire RED Anger Rudolph's nose
Sand between your toes BROWN Bare branches A football
$5 Bill An empty sky BLUE Feeling lonely A bird
Amethyst PURPLE Frozen Toes Grapes
Christmas WHITE Arctic Hare

POETIC POWER!

Activity 11

Parodies

Parodies are poems that imitate familiar poems in a funny way. They begin the same way but have a humorous twist to the ending. For example - Do you remember the nursery rhyme about Humpty Dumpty which goes like this?

> **Humpty Dumpty sat on a wall.**
> **Humpty Dumpty had a great fall.**
> **All the King's horses and all the King's men**
> **Couldn't put Humpty together again.**

A parody of this traditional poem may read like this:

> **Humpty Dumpty sat on a wall.**
> **Humpty Dumpty had a great fall.**
> **All the King's horses and all the King's men.**
> **Had Eggs Benedict for brunch again.**

Read more nursery rhymes - Jack and Jill, Old Mother Hubbard, Hickory Dickory Dock, Jack Be Nimble, etc. - write your own parody. Remember to change only the <u>last</u> line.

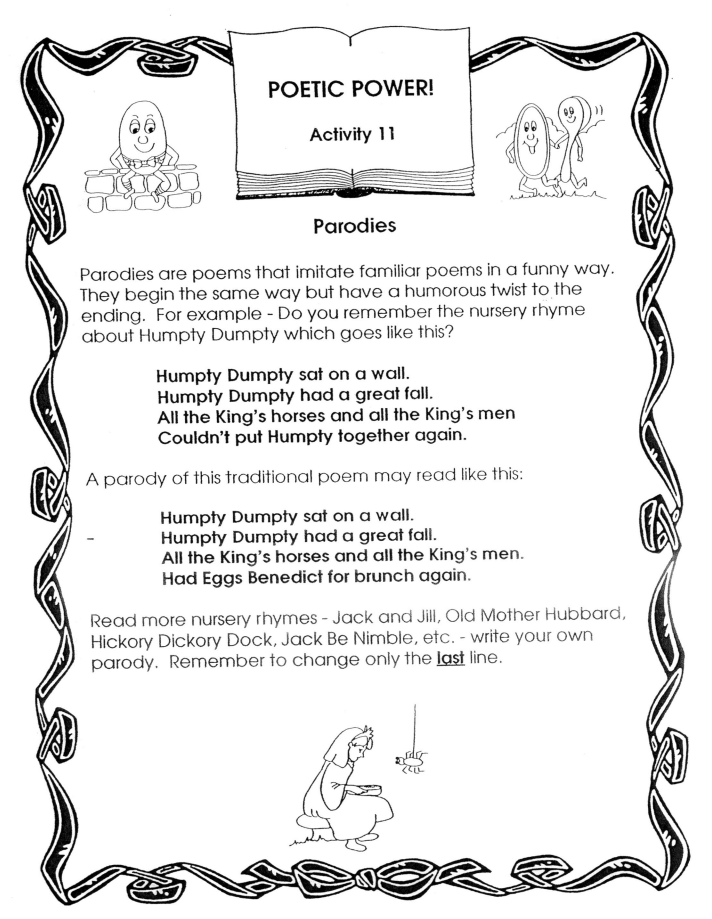

POETIC POWER!

Activity 12

Poems a Poppin'

Did you know that the largest popcorn company in the world is The House of Clarks Ltd. in England which produces 60 million packages of popcorn in one year?

Scientists have found kernels of popcorn that are nearly 4000 years old!

Some popcorn kernels pop as high as 1 meter (1 yard) in the air!

More popcorn was sold during the "Star Wars" movie than during any other.

These popcorn facts may help get you started writing a poem about popcorn. You may also want to pop some corn and describe the smell, sound, feel and taste of the popping corn. In your poem, make use of comparisons and words that appeal to the senses. You may want to write two or three poems and have a classmate choose the most "pop"-ular one to put on display.

WRITING POWER!

Creative Writing

In this section, encourage the students to enrich their story writing by incorporating many of the concepts they learned while creating their own poetry (i.e. similes, metaphors, personification etc.)

WRITING POWER!

Activity 1

The Elements of a Good Story

To cook an appetizing dish, it's important to follow the directions in the recipe. To cook up a delightful story, one must also adhere to a plan or set of guidelines that promote the organization of your ideas in a sequential manner. If you leave out an important ingredient in the recipe, the end result is not always delectable. Likewise, omitting an important element in your story also results in a product of lesser quality.

To write a captivating story follow the "recipe" below.

1. Plan your story with the utmost care. Be sure to use interesting characters and intriguing problems. Make sure your solution is sensible and reasonable.

2. Introduce your characters and their problems near the beginning of the story.

3. Build up your story until it reaches a <u>climax</u> - (the high point = the peak - the most exciting part of any story).

4. Next, reveal the solution(s) to the problem or problems in your story.

5. Finally, make up a good ending. The ending most often makes a comment about the end result of the story. It can be a personal opinion, a moral or a suggestion. This tends to tie together loose ends and gives your story a finishing touch.

See the diagram below:

```
                                    Climax
 Characters                                
 Beginning      Problem      to  /      Solve
                                 /        the
                         Build         Problems        Ending
```

WRITING   POWER!

A Now that you are familiar with the elements of a good story, read the following sentences and decide which part of the story each represents. Put your answers in the blanks provided.

1. With sadness in her heart, Michelle returned home and I'm certain she will not be so anxious to visit old, historic castles again. _____

2. Michelle invited Nancy, her wealthy best friend, to join her on a European vacation where they would be staying in an old English castle. _____

3. Michelle was terrified. Her dream vacation was now a nightmare. She notified Nancy's parents of the disaster. Then she hustled about getting her things packed so she could escape this doomed castle. Anna came into Michelle's room to water the plants and accidently toppled one over. While bending to clean up the mess, Michelle noticed a gun fall from her apron pocket. Michelle pretended not to see this. As soon as Anna left, Michelle notified the police and before long Anna was found guilty of murder and theft.
_____

4. Soon, forgetting about the unlocked window, the adventurous two some embarked on a day of sightseeing. However, before long, as they hurried along home due to the impending storm, Nancy noticed that she and Michelle were being followed. They hastened their steps. _____

5. Soon they were safely inside the castle walls. Thunder roared; the lights flickered, then dimmed and finally, as darkness prevailed, the gunshot shattered the eerie silence in the spooky mansion - Nancy was dead and her diamond necklace was gone._____

6. The first morning, when Michelle and Nancy awoke, their bedroom window was open, much to their dismay, as they were certain that Anna, the maid, had locked it the previous night._____

WRITING POWER!

B Now write this story in sequential order, using paragraph formation.

A Mysterious Vacation

_____

_____

_____

_____

_____

_____

_____

_____

_____

_____

_____

_____

_____

_____

_____

_____

_____

_____

_____

_____

_____

_____

_____

_____

_____

_____

_____

_____

_____

_____

_____

_____

WRITING POWER!

The Elements of a Good Story

Answer Key

(teacher's use only)

A   1. ending

      2. beginning (characters)

      3. solving the problems

      4. building to climax

      5. climax

      6. problem

B   Order of Sentences for Story

        2

        6

        4

        5

        3

        1

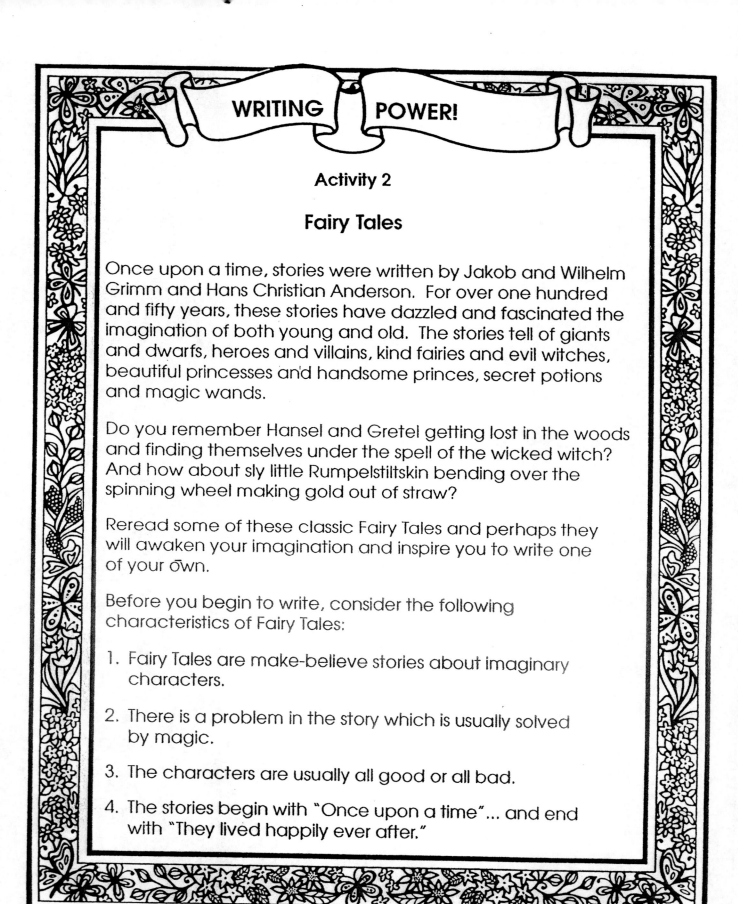

WRITING POWER!

Activity 2

Fairy Tales

Once upon a time, stories were written by Jakob and Wilhelm Grimm and Hans Christian Anderson. For over one hundred and fifty years, these stories have dazzled and fascinated the imagination of both young and old. The stories tell of giants and dwarfs, heroes and villains, kind fairies and evil witches, beautiful princesses and handsome princes, secret potions and magic wands.

Do you remember Hansel and Gretel getting lost in the woods and finding themselves under the spell of the wicked witch? And how about sly little Rumpelstiltskin bending over the spinning wheel making gold out of straw?

Reread some of these classic Fairy Tales and perhaps they will awaken your imagination and inspire you to write one of your own.

Before you begin to write, consider the following characteristics of Fairy Tales:

1. Fairy Tales are make-believe stories about imaginary characters.

2. There is a problem in the story which is usually solved by magic.

3. The characters are usually all good or all bad.

4. The stories begin with "Once upon a time"... and end with "They lived happily ever after."

WRITING POWER!

Activity 2

Fairy Tales

Now write your story and enter a world of illusion where fantasy and wishes will enable you to ride to your castle in the air.

You may wish to choose one of the following titles, or use one of your own.

The Enchanted Castle

Mirror, Mirror on the Wall

Abracadabra

Fairy Dust

The Spell-binding Witch

WRITING POWER!

Activity 3

Adventure Stories

Exciting, thrilling, challenging - all of these words describe an adventure story. Adventure stories have several unique characteristics.

1. The story may be make-believe or real

2. The characters are almost always people.

3. The climax should be very exciting and the end result should come quickly.

Combining your knowledge of what a good story entails with the characteristics outlined above, write an adventure story about <u>one</u> of the following:

1. **I Finally Joined The Circus**

2. **The Adventures of the Lost Penny**

3. **My Trip Around The World**

4. **My Journey into Space**

5. **My Jungle Adventure**

6. **A title of your own choosing**

WRITING POWER!

Activity 4

Fables

Aesop was a Greek slave who lived over 2000 years ago. He was skilled at telling wise, witty tales about animals having human traits. Aesop's fables have remained popular over the years.

Remember "The Fox and the Grapes"? This fable tells of a Fox wanting to eat a bunch of grapes on a vine. When he realized he couldn't reach them, he decided they were probably sour anyway. Today the expression "sour grapes" means that people express a dislike for something they cannot have.

In "The Hare and the Tortoise" we read that the Hare thought he could outrun anyone but we learn from the Tortoise plodding along, that persistence can be more important than speed.

Read many of Aesop's Fables such as

"The Ant and the Grasshopper"
"The Wolf in Sheep's Clothing"
"The Fox and the Crow"
"The City Mouse and the Country Mouse"
"The Crow and the Pitcher"

Then try your hand at writing your own "fab"- ulous fable.
Keep the following characteristics of Fables in mind as you write:

WRITING POWER!

Activity 4

Fables

1. Fables are usually brief, fictitious stories that teach a lesson, or moral.

2. The characters are usually animals that act like people.

3. The lesson is told at the end of the story.

You may want to base your Fable on one of the following wise sayings:

Look before you leap.

Actions speak louder than words.

The race isn't always to the swift.

Honesty is the best policy.

There's a time for work and a time for play.

WRITING POWER!

Activity 5

It's a Mystery To Me

Have you ever experienced the suspense and mounting excitement of an enthralling murder mystery? Mysteries can be so effective that the reader is ready to pounce if anyone shouts "Boo"!

To write a good mystery one must understand the characteristics of a good mystery story.

1. A mystery is a story about something secretive or unexplained. For example - a murder, a theft etc.

2. The characters are almost always people.

3. Before the climax is reached, clues must be given that hint toward the solution of the problem.

4. The story's excitement should mount as it reaches - the climax.

5. Once the mystery is solved, the story should end quickly.

Select <u>one</u> of the following titles and write a captivating thriller!

1. **The Secret of The Old Attic**

2. **The Hidden Staircase To The Unknown**

3. **The Mystery of The Old Abandoned Pirate's Inn**

4. **The Picture With The Moving Eyes**

5. **The Mysterious Noises In The School Cafeteria**

WRITING POWER!

Activity 6

Tall Tales

Paul Bunyan was an imaginary hero who is supposed to have lived over one hundred years ago in a lumber camp. The men who worked in these camps were called lumberjacks and they used to sit around the campfire at night and tell "tall tales" about Paul Bunyan and Babe, his great blue ox. Paul was a great giant, the biggest lumberjack of all, and he did many wonderfully impossible things. Almost everything in the stories about Paul Bunyan and Babe is made up. Try to read some of the exciting and amusing stories about Paul Bunyan before writing a tall tale of your own.

Read the following characteristics of tall tales then s - t - r - e - t - c - h your imagination and write a believable unbelievable tale of your own.

1. A tall tale begins in a believable way, but it grows and grows.

2. The characters may be real or make-believe.

3. There is usually a problem which is solved in a surprising or unusual way.

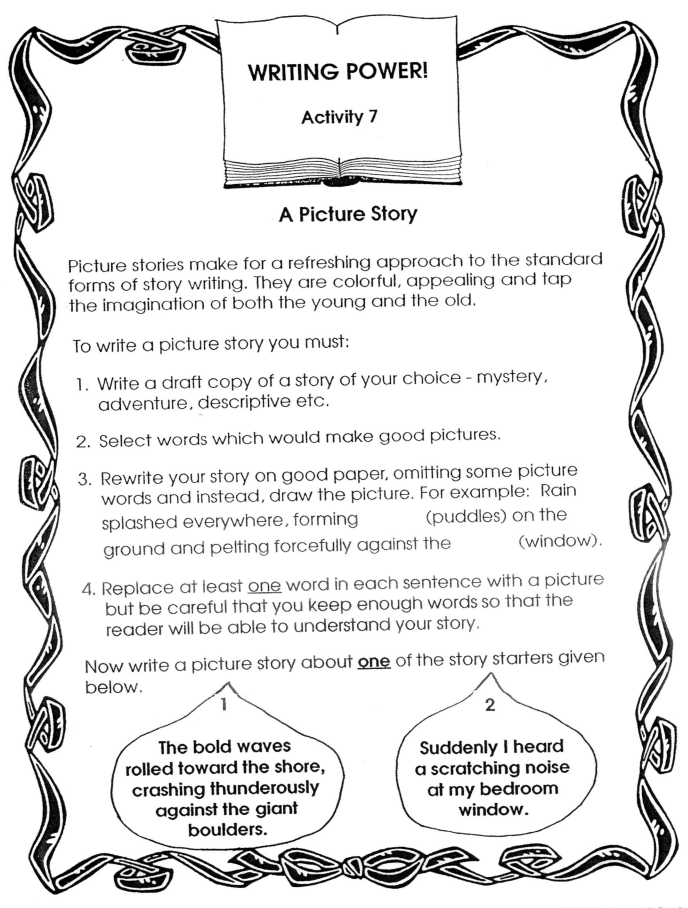

WRITING POWER!

Activity 7

A Picture Story

Picture stories make for a refreshing approach to the standard forms of story writing. They are colorful, appealing and tap the imagination of both the young and the old.

To write a picture story you must:

1. Write a draft copy of a story of your choice - mystery, adventure, descriptive etc.

2. Select words which would make good pictures.

3. Rewrite your story on good paper, omitting some picture words and instead, draw the picture. For example: Rain splashed everywhere, forming   (puddles) on the ground and pelting forcefully against the   (window).

4. Replace at least <u>one</u> word in each sentence with a picture but be careful that you keep enough words so that the reader will be able to understand your story.

Now write a picture story about <u>one</u> of the story starters given below.

1

The bold waves rolled toward the shore, crashing thunderously against the giant boulders.

2

Suddenly I heard a scratching noise at my bedroom window.

WRITING POWER!

Activity 7

A Picture Story

3

As I walked along in the cold, damp darkness, I could hear footsteps coming behind me.

4

John knew that if his parents found out, he would be punished but there was no turning back now.

5

The children laughed uncontrollably as the monkey entertained them.

6

My suitcase was packed and I shook with excitement just thinking that in one hour I would be on my way to Europe.

WRITING POWER!

Activity 8

Animal Stories

Animals have long been the topic about which man has written stories. The subjects range from meek little mice to massive elephants, from the desert rat to the Arctic fox, from farm animals to jungle animals. Many people are intrigued by cats of any size, while others favor dogs, and still others are enthralled by marine animals

No matter what the choice, the writer must follow certain criteria for writing animal stories.

1. The main characters are animals.
2. These stories may be real or make-believe.
3. The author must know many facts about the animals.
4. If the story is make-believe, the animals talk and act like people.

Choose an animal that will be the main character in your story. Do some research to find out about its habits and behavior before you begin.

I'm sure you have the "purr" - fect animal in mind.

WRITING POWER!

Activity 9

A S-M-A-S-H-ing Story

A 1. Pick any number from 1 to 10. _____

2. Write down any two of your favorite people.

_____   _____

3. Pick any year - past or future. _____

4. Select any age. _____

5. Select any country in the world. _____

6. Pick a letter from M-A-S-H. _____

B The following sentences explain the above choices.

1. This is the number of words in the title of your story.

2. These are the two main characters in your story.

3. This is the year that your story takes place.

4. This is the age of the people in your story.

5. This is the country where your story takes place.

6. If you chose: **M**- you write a mystery story.
   A - you write an adventure story.
   S - you write a serious or science fiction story.
   H - you write a horror or a humorous story.

Have fun. I'm sure your story will be a **S-M-A-S-H-ing** success!

WRITING POWER!

Activity 10

A Star is Born

Pretend you are a star - a star football player, a prima ballerina, a lead singer in a rock group, an actor in the movies or on T.V.

What is your life like as a star? Write about it in the shape below.

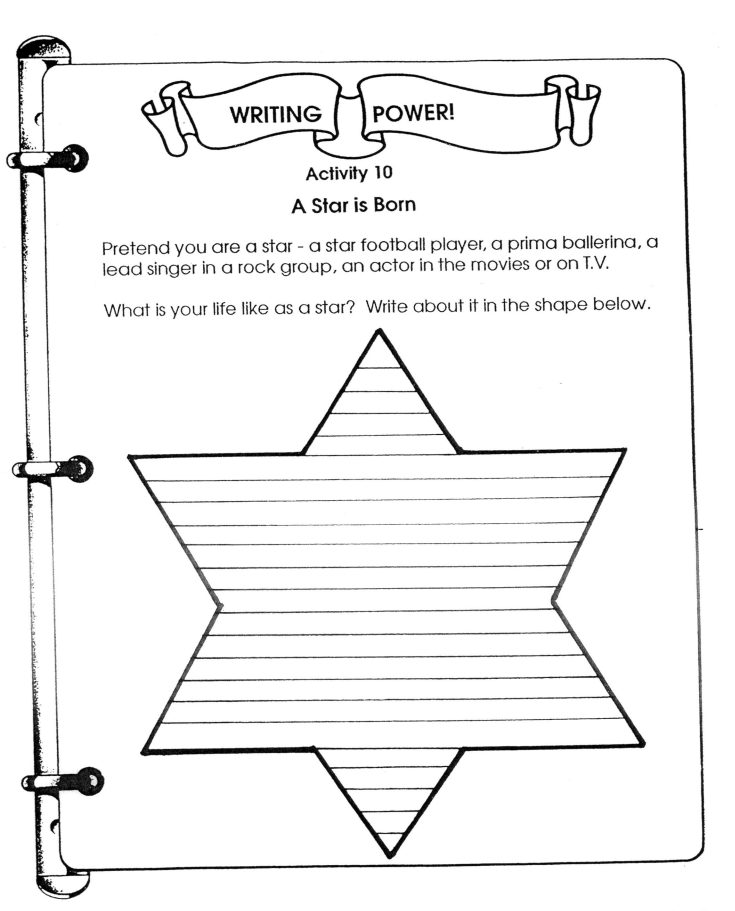

WRITING POWER!

Activity 11

The "Tall" and the "Short" Of It.

When Lewis Carroll wrote **Alice In Wonderland** he created a classic. Whether we read the story or watch it come to life on the "big screen", it is still a source of enjoyment for children of all ages.

I'm sure you recall the part when Alice drinks a potion and suddenly shrinks to the size of a thimble.

Pretend you are 145 cm (57 in.) tall.

Just imagine if one morning you woke up and realized, to your horror, that you were now only 2 cm (1 in.) tall.

What would you do?

How would you feel?

Imagine the reaction of your parents, siblings, friends and classmates.

How would you cope with all the changes you must make in your life?

Tell your story!

Let your imagination soar.

Don't "short" change your readers!

WRITING POWER!

Activity 12

Sailing, Sailing

If you could stop everything you are doing and could sail anywhere in the world for three months, where would you go?

What kinds of adventures might you have on the high seas?

If you were permitted to take only one person with you, who would it be? Why?

Brainstorm for some sailing words, write them on the boat shape, and be a dreamer as you write your story and sail off into the sunset.

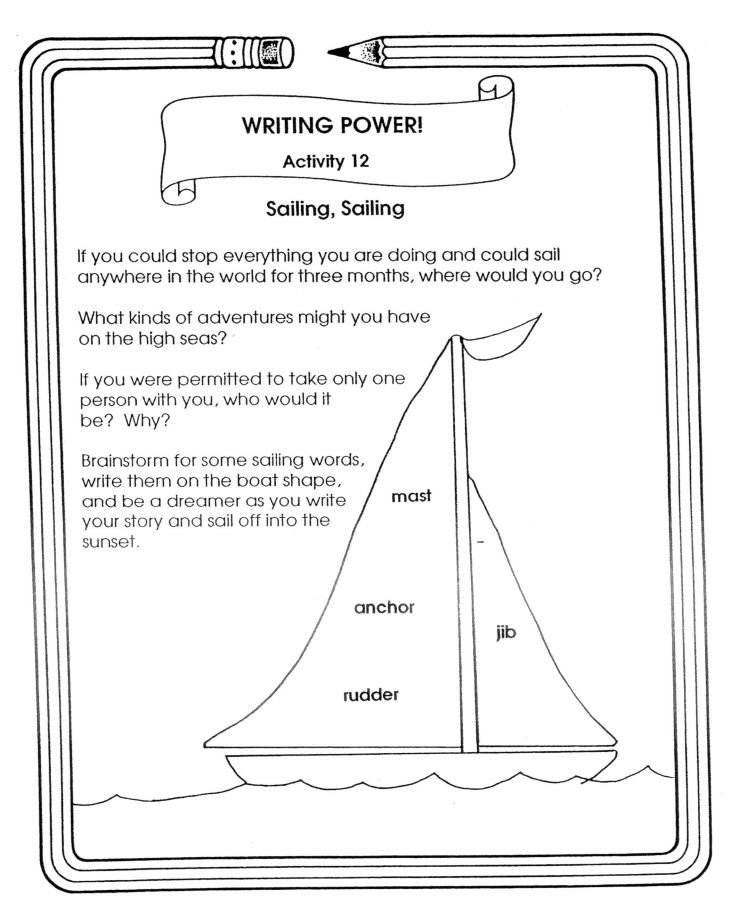

mast

anchor

jib

rudder

WRITING POWER!

Activity 13

Somewhere Over the Rainbow

Perhaps you have heard the song "Somewhere Over The Rainbow" sung by Judy Garland who played Dorothy in The Wizard of Oz.

Have you ever wondered if there really is a pot of gold at the end of the rainbow?

Pretend that a magical power enables you to follow the rainbow to its end and there you find something far greater than gold.

There lies before you a land where dreams come true.

What does this land look like?
Who lives there?
What happens in this land?
How do dreams come true?

What secret magic is responsible for this land of glorious bliss? Describe your experiences in this land of dreams come true!

May your every wish be granted!

WRITING POWER!

Activity 14

Cook Up a Story

Stir up your imagination, add <u>one</u> ingredient from each of the lists below, and mix together to cook up a yummy tale to feast upon.

WHO		**WHERE**	
you	your best pal	in a jet	in the kitchen
your pet	a dinosaur	on a raft	on the beach
a robot	an invisible man	at a circus	on an island
friends	an old woman	on the moon	in the forest
Batman	the Joker	at school	in a tree house

WHEN		**WHAT**	
long ago	midnight	an accident	a computer
sometime	yesterday	an old chest	a skeleton
now	the year 2020	a cobra	a great day
tomorrow	your birthday	a party	a flat tire
Hallowe'en	Christmas	a souvenir	a footprint

WRITING POWER!

Activity 15

From Dull to Dazzling Descriptions

If you incorporate good, descriptive writing when composing your stories, it can alter your end results from dull to dazzling! Description makes your stories come to life. It makes the reader see, hear, feel, taste and touch what you describe.

Example: **A description of a snowfall at night:**

A peaceful serenity encompassed the land, as the dancing snowflakes twirled and tumbled on their journey to the frozen land below. The pure white snow carpeted the earth. The light from the moon made the new fallen snow dazzle and sparkle like diamonds. It was a glorious sight to behold.

Write your own descriptions about the topics given below:

a newborn baby	_____

a sunset	_____

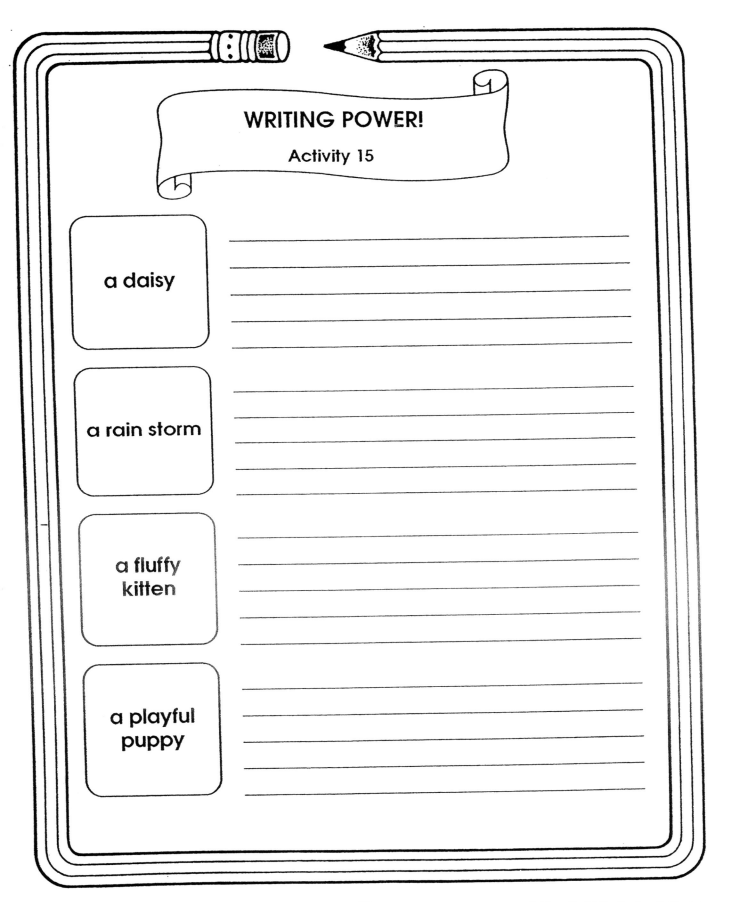

WRITING POWER!

Activity 15

a daisy

a rain storm

a fluffy kitten

a playful puppy

WRITING POWER!

Activity 16

A "Tree"-mendous Story

You are walking through the forest one day. In a clearing you find a magic tree.

Write a "tree"-mendous story telling about this tree in all its splendor.

Before starting your story, brainstorm and write ten appropriate words in the tree shape. After your story is written, draw a picture showing what your magic tree looks like.

WRITING POWER!

Activity 17

A Chinese Mystery

The diagram below is an old Chinese puzzle called a tangram.
The tangram has 7 pieces: 5 triangles, 1 square and 1 rhomboid
(a parallelogram with unequal sides).

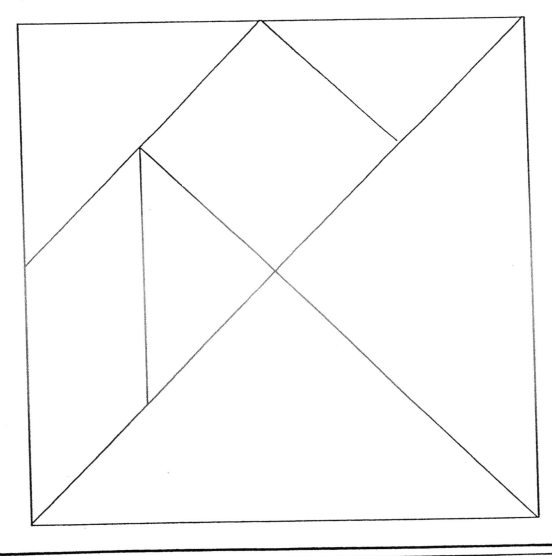

WRITING POWER!

Activity 17

A Chinese Mystery

Now you're going to write a story of your choice. Here's how!

1. To begin your story first write a draft copy on lined paper. When you are pleased with your editing, you are ready to proceed.

2. Cut out the tangram pieces and put them in an envelope.

3. Randomly select one piece at a time and write your story on the pieces. Put them back in the envelope.

4. Trade envelopes with a partner. Then glue the tangram pieces together on a piece of construction paper.

5. Read the story segments carefully. Then number them from 1 to 7 in sequential order.

6. Upon completion, pass the finished product back to your partner to see if you sequenced the story correctly.

Did you solve the Chinese mystery?

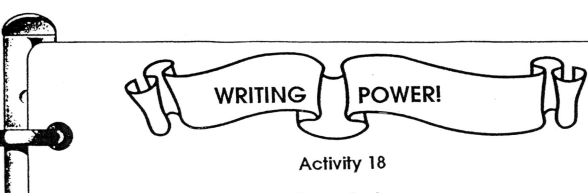

WRITING POWER!

Activity 18

Tuned - In

Write a letter to the manager of your local television station. In the letter tell him what your favorite T.V. show is and why you like it so much.

Also tell him what show you do not like and give reasons why you think it shouldn't be aired.

Get tuned-in and do a good job.

 OTM-1803 • SSR1-03 How To Write Poetry & Stories

WRITING POWER!

Activity 19
Creative Sentences

I Alliteration: Take any letter of the alphabet and write a sentence having each word begin with that particular letter.

Example: **Wee Willy was Whittling within Wilfred's wigwam.**

II Challenge! Here's a sentence containing <u>**all**</u> the letters of the alphabet.

The quick brown fox jumps over the lazy dog.

Now you try writing a sentence containing as many of the 26 letters as you possibly can.

III Words of Interest: Some interesting words have the following double-letters.

double <u>a</u> - baz<u>aa</u>r, <u>aa</u>rdvark
double <u>h</u> - hig<u>hh</u>anded
double <u>i</u> - ski<u>i</u>ng
double <u>k</u> - boo<u>kk</u>eeper, jac<u>kk</u>nife
double <u>u</u> - vac<u>uu</u>m
double <u>v</u> - fli<u>vv</u>er
double <u>w</u> - po<u>ww</u>ow
double <u>z</u> - ja<u>zz</u>ing, pu<u>zz</u>le, di<u>zz</u>y

Choose any <u>five</u> of the above words and use them in interesting sentences.

WRITING POWER!

Activity 19

Creative Sentences

IV "dous" words: There are only five descriptive words ending in "dous" in common use.
They are:

> **tremendous**
> **hazardous**
> **horrendous**
> **stupendous**
> **jeopardous**

Use each word in a creative interesting sentence. Check your dictionary first if you don't know their meanings.

Do a stupendous job!

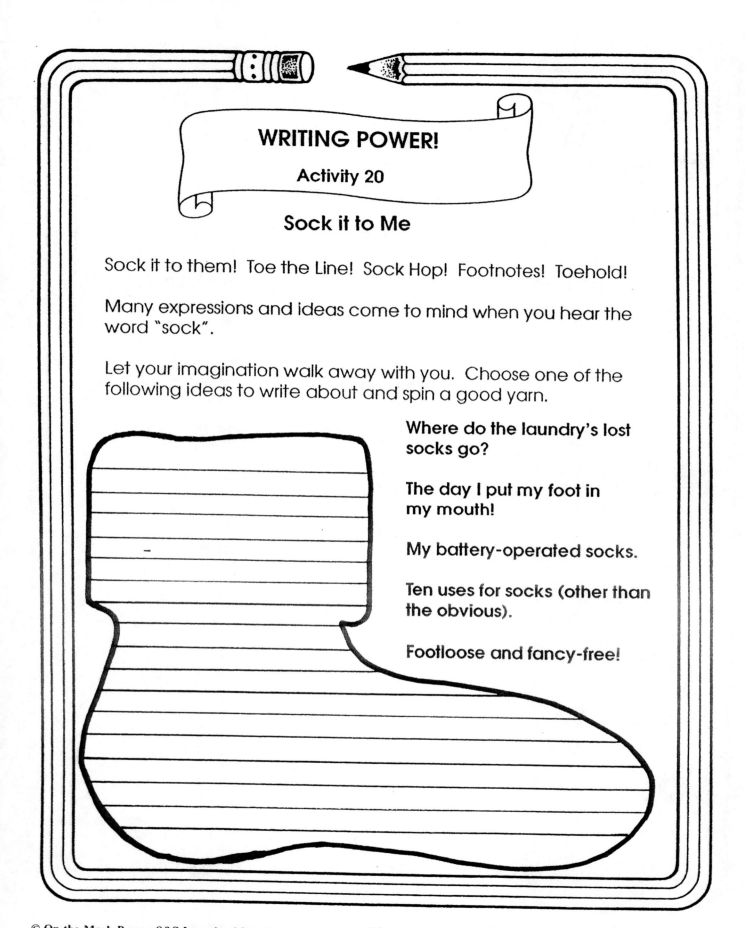

WRITING POWER!

Activity 20

Sock it to Me

Sock it to them! Toe the Line! Sock Hop! Footnotes! Toehold!

Many expressions and ideas come to mind when you hear the word "sock".

Let your imagination walk away with you. Choose one of the following ideas to write about and spin a good yarn.

Where do the laundry's lost socks go?

The day I put my foot in my mouth!

My battery-operated socks.

Ten uses for socks (other than the obvious).

Footloose and fancy-free!

WRITING POWER!

Activity 21

A Picture is Worth a Thousand Words

Look through magazines for
pictures that you could use for story writing.

Choose **one** that interests you and in a thousand words
(or less) tell a story about what **you** think is happening.

Describe the setting, the characters, plot, climax, and
the ending.

Mount the magazine picture and your story on a piece
of sturdy paper or cardboard.

Put your story on display.

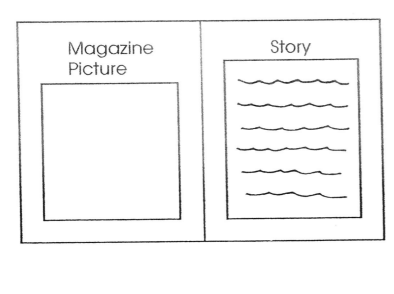

Magazine Picture	Story

WRITING POWER!

Activity 22

The Big Scoop

Imagine that you are opening an ice cream parlor. You want to "lick" everyone else in the business by being creative and offering a flavor of ice cream for **every** letter of the alphabet

Write 26 scooper-dooper flavors below.

Read Shel Silverstein's poem "Eighteen Flavors" for some motivation.

A _____

B bubble gum

C _____

D _____

E _____

F _____

G _____

H _____

J _____

K _____

L _____

M marshmallow
madness

N _____

O _____

P pizza ripple

Q _____

R rocky road

S _____

T tutti frutti

U _____

V _____

W _____

X _____

Y _____

Z _____

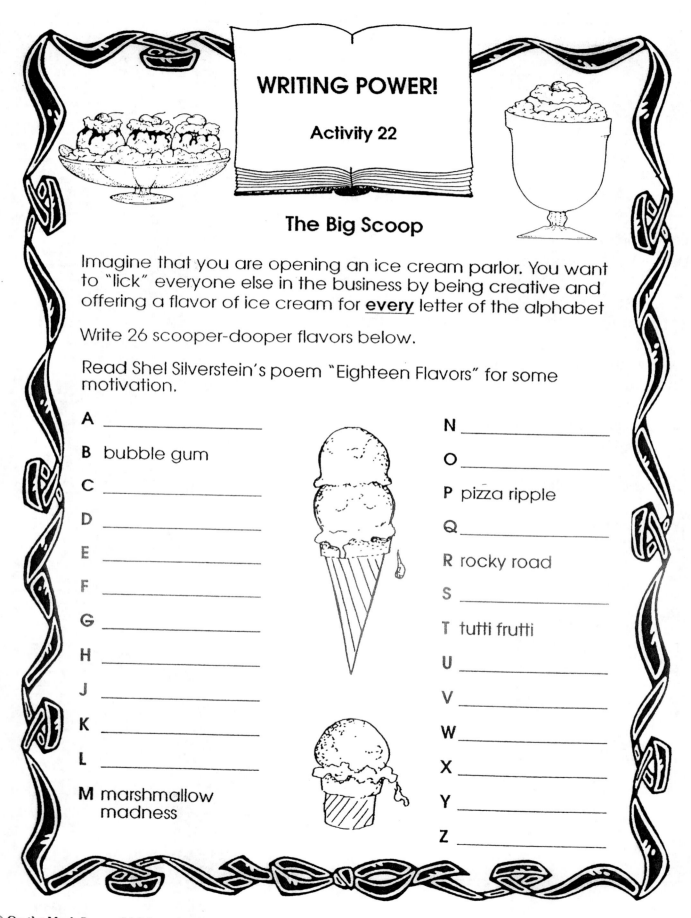

WRITING POWER!

Activity 23

Great Beginnings

The sentences below offer great beginnings for stories. But what about the endings? When we go to a movie or read a good book we wait in anticipation for the ending to come. Sometimes there is a happy ending, but if a character doesn't solve the problem there is an unhappy ending.

You be the storyteller. It is up to you to choose **one** of the beginnings and write an interesting ending. There is no need to write on "end"-lessly. Get right to the point and make it "end"-eresting.

Beginnings:

1. I had been offered $10.00 to sleep alone in the cemetery all night. I placed my sleeping bag on the ground near a large tombstone. I crawled into it and closed my eyes. Suddenly I heard a groan ...

2. The minute I accepted the dare I knew I had made a big mistake. My friends dared me to swim across Great Lake and I was going to prove I wasn't chicken. Now I was exhausted with more than half the distance to go and my muscles ached...

3. Dad was an excellent pilot, but when I heard the sputter of the engine I knew our only hope was to bail out. After jumping, I pulled the rip cord -- it didn't open ...

WRITING POWER!

Activity 23

Great Beginnings

4. Camping with my family is always fun but this one particular time it turned out to be more fun than I had bargained for. After arriving at the campsite, I decided to go for a walk. Some luscious red berries caught my eye and I started to eat them. I leaned against a pine tree and it toppled over! I discovered I had super human strength ...

5. One day I was riding my bicycle down Main Street. As I approached the bank, a man carrying a large bag was running towards me. Suddenly a policeman shouted, "Stop that thief!" ...

WRITING POWER!

Activity 24

An Inquiring Mind

The greatest stories are usually the product of an inquiring mind. When writing a story, you should first brainstorm and ask yourself a number of imperative questions.

1. **Where** could my story take place? - on a desert, a sandy beach or deep in the chilly Arctic? Perhaps you could list several and then choose the one best suited to your story.

2. **What** type of people and/or animals are most suitable for my story? Should your characters be serious or comical, kind or mean, dauntless or deceitful?

3. **When** could my story take place? - the past, the present or the future? Should it take place in the afternoon, at dusk or in the dead of the night?

4. **How** are the weather conditions under which my story takes place? Should there be a raging snow storm, a thunder and lightning storm, a tornado, hurricane or should it be a hot, sultry day?

Read the story starters below. Select **one** and answer the where, what, when and how questions about your topic.

Story Starters

1. There it was - the old sea chest that I had hunted ardently to find.

2. Horror shuttered my being, as I discovered that my expensive heirloom brooch was missing.

WRITING POWER!

Activity 24

An Inquiring Mind

3. I waited and waited but my parents did not show up - what happened? Where could they be?

4. I was walking along when suddenly the building across the street exploded into flames.

5. I was creeping along, uncertain of my step, when to my horror I suddenly fell through the trap door!

The story starter I chose is:

_____

_____

_____

Give several answers for each question.

1. Where could this story take place?

_____

_____

_____

2. What type of animals or people are best suited for this story?

_____

_____

_____

3. When could this story take place?

_____

_____

_____

WRITING POWER!

Activity 24

An Inquiring Mind

4. How should the weather conditions be, when this story takes place?

_____

_____

_____

Now compile some of your brainstorming ideas into an original, imaginative story of your own. Give your story a catchy title!

_____

_____

_____

_____

_____

_____

_____

_____

_____

_____

_____

_____

_____

_____

_____

_____

_____

_____

_____

Creative Writing Award

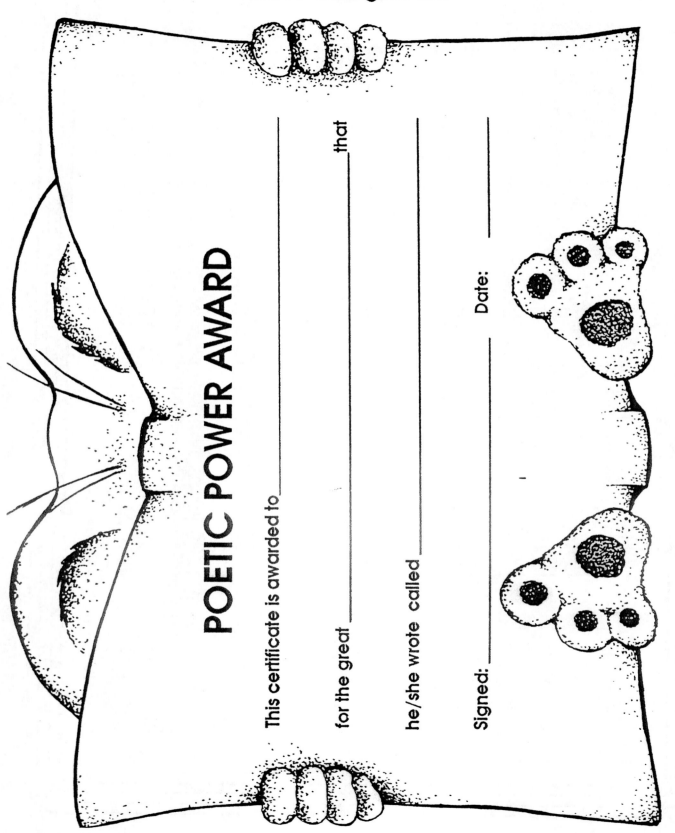

POETIC POWER AWARD

This certificate is awarded to

that

for the great

he/she wrote called

Signed:

Date:

OTM-1803 • SSR1-03 How To Write Poetry & Stories

Creative Writing Award

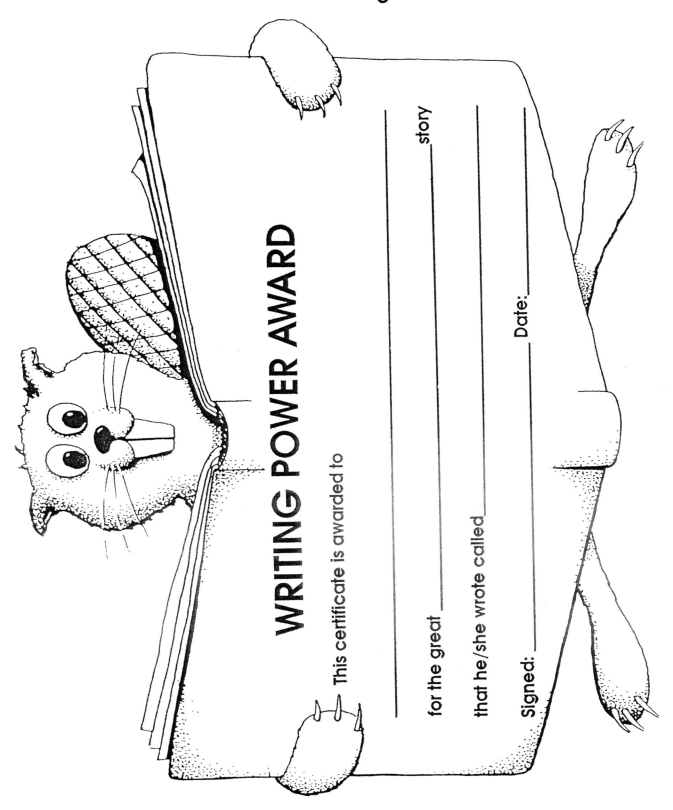

WRITING POWER AWARD

This certificate is awarded to

_____

for the great _____ story

that he/she wrote called _____

Signed: _____

Date: _____

60

OTM-1803 • SSR1-03 How To Write Poetry & Stories